Discovering God's World
Science Reader

Third Edition

by Judy Hull Moore

A Beka Book® Pensacola, FL 32523-9100
an affiliated ministry of PENSACOLA CHRISTIAN COLLEGE®

A Beka Book
Science and Health Series

Science

K   God's World
Grade 1   Discovering God's World
2   Enjoying God's World
3   Exploring God's World
4   Understanding God's World
5   Investigating God's World
6   Observing God's World

Health

- Health, Safety, and Manners 1
- Health, Safety, and Manners 2
- Health, Safety, and Manners 3
- Developing Good Health
- Enjoying Good Health
- Choosing Good Health

Discovering God's World Science Reader
Third Edition

Staff Credits
Editors: Laurel Hicks, Naomi Sleeth
Designer: Mark Whitcher
Production Artist: Tracey Malone
Illustrators: Brian Jekel, Paul De Luna, Jason Atwell, Stephanie Blatch

A Beka Book, a Christian textbook ministry affiliated with Pensacola Christian College, is designed to meet the need for Christian textbooks and teaching aids. The purpose of this publishing ministry is to help Christian schools reach children and young people for the Lord and train them in the Christian way of life.

"I Can Be Anyone" by Adele H. Seronde is reprinted by permission of McGraw-Hill Inc. from *Basic Reading, Book C* by Glenn McCracken and Charles C. Walcutt. Copyright © 1975, 1969, 1963 by J. B. Lippincott Company.

Photo locations are identified by the following abbreviations: t—top, b—bottom, c—center, l—left, r—right. Those not credited are the property of the publisher.

Discovering God's World
Moore, Judy Hull.
        Discovering God's world: science reader / by Judy
    Hull Moore; edited by Laurel Hicks, Naomi Sleeth. — 3rd ed.
        129 p.; col. ill.; 28 cm. (A Beka Book science and health series)
        1. Science — Study and teaching (Primary) 2. Readers (Primary)
III. Hicks, Laurel.   IV. Sleeth, Naomi.   V. A Beka Book, Inc.
Library of Congress: Q161.2 .M66 1995
Dewey System: 500

Animals, Animals. Inc.: 50 b—James D. Watt; 56 tr—Robert Maier, br—Zig Leszczynski; 73 t—Zig Leszczynski; 88 r—Richard LaVal; 89—J. A. L. Cooke/Oxford Scientific Films. **Courtesy Corel Corporation:** cover, title page: duck, butterfly, leaf, orchids, bug, elephant, iv, 1 lb, 3: third from tr, 9 bl, 23: food, 46, 47 r, 48, 49, 52 r, 56 tl, 59: except baby rabbits, 61, 62, 64, 65, 67, 70, 71, 72, 74, 75, 76, 77, 79: except tl, 80, 81, 84, 85 except c, 94, 95, 96, 99, 102, 106, 107, 110, 112, 113, 114, 119, 121, 122, 123, 126, 128, 130–131. **Courtesy Corbis:** cover, title page: sunflower; 1 t; 3: except 3rd from tr, 4, 9: except bl, 13, 14, 15, 23 tl, 26, 27, 29, 30, 47 l, 98 b, 108. **Courtesy Mountain High Maps,** copyright © 1993 Digital Wisdom, Inc.: page 4 globe. **Photo Researchers, Inc.:** 50 t—Tom McHugh, c—Merlin D. Tuttle/Bat Conservation International; 51—Leonard Lee Rue III; 52 l—Leonard Lee Rue III; 53—Mike James; 54—Tom McHugh; 56 bl—J. H. Robinson; 59 baby rabbits—J. H. Robinson; 66—J. Durk/Okapia; 73 b—Gregory K. Scott; 85 c—Scott Camazine; 87—J. P. Varin/Jacana; 88 l—Scott Camazine; 90—Dr. Paul A. Zahl; 91—N. H. (Dan) Cheatham; 92—Scott Camazine. **Western Marine Laboratory:** 79 tl.

Contents

 SOMETHING TO TRY

Discovering Insects 79

SOMETHING TO TRY

HANDS ON activity SOMETHING TO TRY
Find a baby plant and watch
it grow 101
Make some funny planters 103
Grow a plant from a root 105
Watch water rise up a stem 106

HANDS ON activity SOMETHING TO TRY
Bring some twigs to life 115
Find air in water and soil 117
Make a bird feeder 118
Plant a bean garden 120

Discovering
Myself

I Can Be Anyone

I can
    Jump as a robin
I can
    Hum as a bee
I can
    Hop on a twig
As a chick-a-deedee!
I can
    Run as a red fox
I can buzz as a fly—
I can
    be Anyone!
But no one
    Can Be I!

        —Adele H. Seronde

Vocabulary: discovering   anyone

Just think of that! I can pretend to be anything. But no one can be me. God made me very special. I am not like anyone else in the world.

God is interested in me. He is interested in what I do and why I do it.

I am very special to God. He is very special to me.

Vocabulary: interested   special

There are millions of girls and boys in the world. But God made me different from everyone else. He made you different from everyone else, too.

Isn't God wonderful?

Vocabulary: everyone   millions
different   wonderful

My Hands

On each hand I have four fingers and a thumb. Because God gave me these, I can do many things.

I can get dressed.   I can hold things.

I can write.   I can help Mommy.

Vocabulary: fingers

Something to do!

✏️ *Trace your hand.*

Bryce's right hand

I must ask God to help my hands do what is right.

"I will praise thee; for I am fearfully and wonderfully made."

Psalm 139:14

Vocabulary: fearfully   wonderfully

My Fingerprints

If I put my hand on the window, I will see a way God made me different from everyone. When I take my hand away, I see **fingerprints.**

Each finger has a different fingerprint. So I have ten different fingerprints.

Somewhere, there might be someone who looks almost like me. But no one can have fingerprints just like mine.

God made everyone's fingerprints different.

Vocabulary: fingerprints   almost

 **Something to try!**

Be a thumb-print detective.

Are your thumb prints really different from those of your friends? Try this and see!

What you need:

- index card
- pencil
- ink pad
- hand lens
- soap, water, and towel
- some friends

What to do:

1. Write your name on the index card.
2. Roll your right thumb on the ink pad.
3. Roll the thumb onto the card.
4. Wash your hands.
5. Look at your thumb print with a hand lens.
6. Look at your friends' prints.

Does anyone have a thumb print just like yours?

Joseph Evans

Emily   Bryce

Vocabulary:

Vocabulary: detective

My Hair

God made my **hair** just as special as my fingerprints. No one else has hair quite like mine.

Some hair is straight.

Some hair is fine.

Some hair is thick.

Some hair is curly.

Vocabulary: straight   curly

My Hair Grows

All hair grows out of the skin from **roots.** These roots are below the skin. The blood brings food to the hair roots to help the hair grow.

When my hair grows, the roots push the hair up to make it longer.

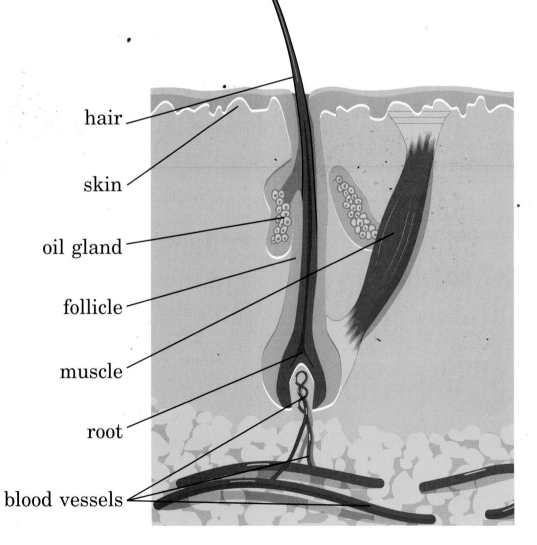

hair

skin

oil gland

follicle

muscle

root

blood vessels

Vocabulary: follicle   muscle

The Color of My Hair

Every hair has **pigment.** There are many pigments—black, brown, red, or yellow. That's why my hair is the color that it is.

Vocabulary: color   pigment

Something to do!

Color each child's hair.

black

brown

yellow

red

How Many Hairs Do I Have?

Do you know that almost everyone has over one hundred thousand hairs on his head?

Do you know our God is so great that He knows the exact number of hairs we have?

No one knows that but God.

The Bible Says,

"But the very hairs of your head are all numbered."

Matthew 10:30

Vocabulary: thousand   numbered

My Eyes

My eyes are one of God's wonderful gifts to me. My eyes tell me what is going on all around me. I use my eyes to read, to work, to have fun, and to find my way around.

God did not place my eyes too close together or too far apart. God put them just far enough apart to let me see things far away and very close at the same time.

Vocabulary: together   enough

God Takes Care of My Eyes

God knew my eyes would be very important to me. When He made them, He planned a way to protect them.

The bones of our head are called the **skull.** The skull helps to keep things from hitting our eyes.

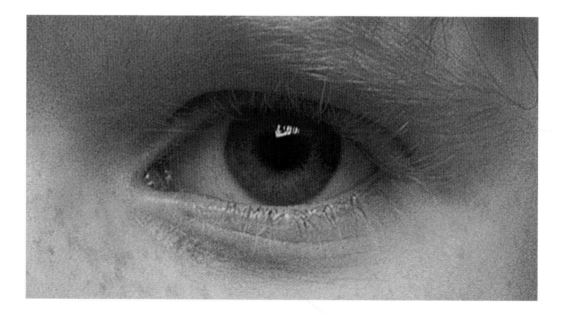

My **eyelids** close to keep dirt and other things from getting into my eyes.

My **eyelashes** keep most dust from getting into my eyes.

Vocabulary: important   eyelashes

Do you know that we always have tears in our eyes, even when we are not crying? Tears keep our eyes moist. When things get in our eyes, tears wash them away.

If I try to keep my eyes open for a very long time, they will sting. That's because my tears have dried up.

Now I will blink my eyes. When I blink, my eyelids spread tears over my eyes, and they feel better.

Vocabulary: moist

I Take Care of My Eyes

God is very wise to think of all of this to help me take care of my eyes, isn't He? God expects me to be wise and take good care of what He has given me.

Something to do!

✏️ *Draw lines to match.*

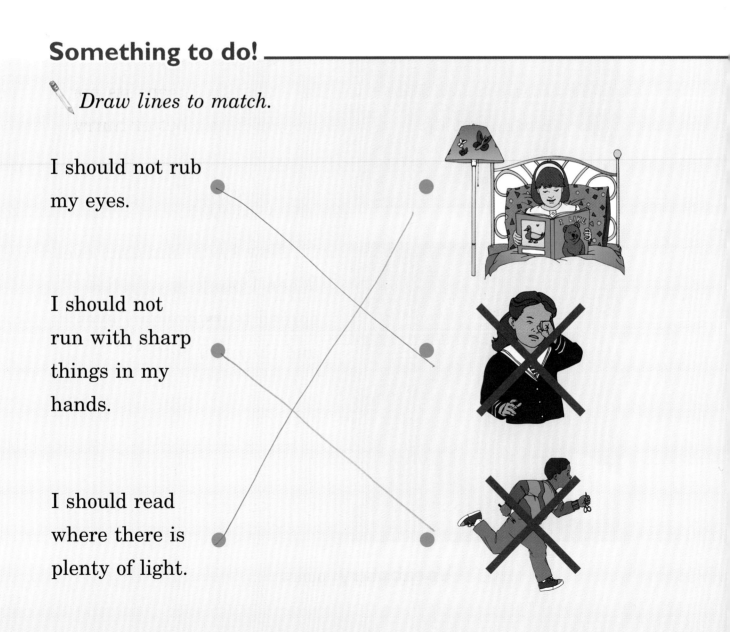

I should not rub my eyes.

I should not run with sharp things in my hands.

I should read where there is plenty of light.

My Ears

Ears are another one of God's wonderful gifts to me.

My alarm clock rings.
I must get up.

The school bus beeps its horn.
I know I had better hurry.

Mother calls goodbye.
I love to hear her voice.

My teacher teaches very
well. I must listen
to what she says.

Vocabulary: listen

My cat purrs when I pet her. I can feel her chest shake. That makes the air shake. The air makes my **eardrum** shake. Now I can hear my cat!

It all happens very, very fast. God made it work this way.

Vocabulary: eardrum   happens

 **Something to try!** _____

Find out how sound travels.

Sound is like the wind. You can't see it, but you can see what it does. Try this and see!

What you need:

- long, thick rubber band
- thin paper
- a friend

What to do:

1. Hold the rubber band with a friend.

2. Pluck the rubber band with your finger as your friend holds the paper close.

The plucked rubber band shakes back and forth. It makes the air shake. The air makes the paper shake. The shaking air reaches your ears, and you hear!

Did you hear the sound? Did you see the paper shake?

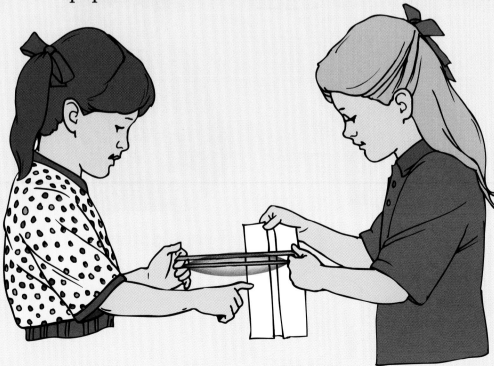

Taking Care of My Ears

I must take good care of my ears,
for there is much to hear and learn.

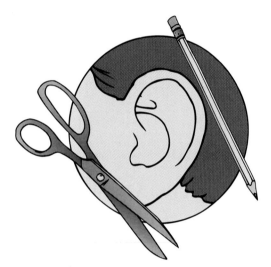

I should keep my ears
warm when the cold
wind blows.

I should never put
anything into my ears.

I should never
let anything hit
my ears.

I should always keep
them clean.

My Nose

My mother just made a chocolate cake. I did not see it, but I can tell. Do you know how?

My nose told me!

The holes in my nose are called **nostrils.** With my nostrils I smell and breathe.

Sometimes I get a cold. I can't use my nose to breathe then. God knew that. He gave me another way to breathe when I can't use my nose. I use my mouth.

Vocabulary: chocolate   nostrils

It is much better to use my nose than my mouth to breathe. Hairs grow in my nostrils. These hairs catch most of the dust from the air I breathe.

Sometimes dust gets past these hairs. Then I sneeze—KER-CHOO! That is God's way for me to get rid of dust and germs.

Vocabulary: germs

My Tongue

Oh, boy! Ice cream! Strawberry is my favorite flavor. What kind do you like best?

If I close my eyes, I can still tell what flavor I am eating.

My tongue is God's wonderful gift to me. God wants me to eat the right food. God also wants me to enjoy that food.

Vocabulary: strawberry   favorite
flavor   tongue

So God put **taste buds** on my tongue. When I eat, my food rolls all over my tongue. Different parts of my tongue tell me if I am eating something sour, salty, bitter, or sweet.

Vocabulary: medicine

Something to do!

Draw lines to match the word with the food.

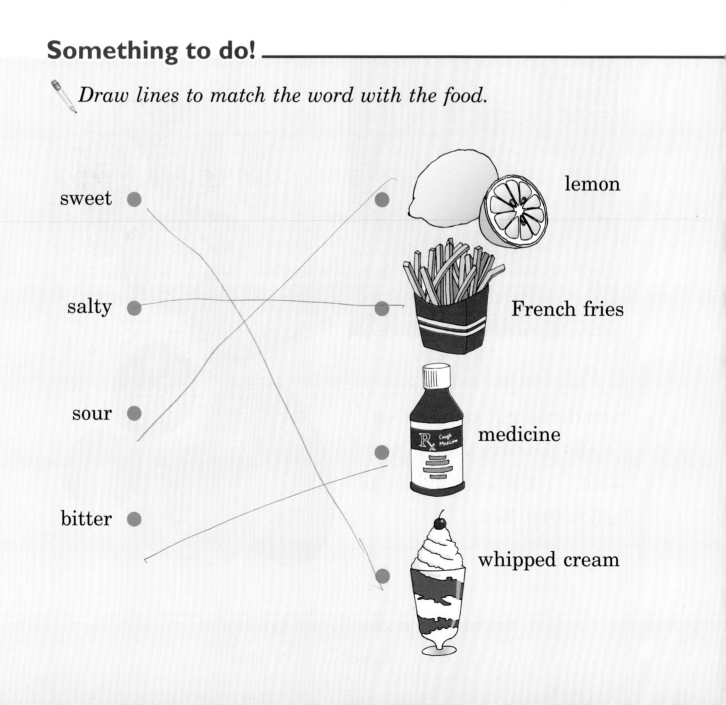

sweet

salty

sour

bitter

lemon

French fries

medicine

whipped cream

 **Something to try!**

Discover how senses work together.

Does your nose help you taste things? Try this and see!

What you need:

- 2" cubes of raw potato and apple
- blindfold
- paper plate

What to do:

1. Wash your hands.
2. Put on the blindfold.
3. Hold your nose.
4. Taste the cubes.
5. Unplug your nose and taste again.

Does your nose help your tongue taste things?

Your tongue can taste only four things—sweet, sour, salty, and bitter. The rest of your taste comes from how a food smells. This is why food does not taste as good when you have a cold!

My Tongue Helps Me to Speak

I also need my tongue to help me form words. I like to talk to people, but I must watch what I say.

My tongue is very little, but what it says can make others happy or sad.

The Bible Says,

"The tongue is a little member, and boasteth great things. Behold, how great a matter a little fire kindleth!"

James 3:5

Vocabulary: boasteth   kindleth

Two and One

I have two ears and only one mouth;
    The reason, I think, is clear:
It teaches me that it will not do
    To talk about all I hear.

I have two eyes and only one mouth;
    The reason of this must be,
That I should learn it will not do
    To talk about all I see.

I have two hands and only one mouth;
    And it is worth repeating:
The two are for work that I need to do—
    The one is for eating.

—*Memory Gems, 1886*

Vocabulary: reason   repeating

My Skin

I like to feel cold, wet snowflakes on my nose.

Mother was afraid I would be cold, so she put nice, warm clothes on me.

My hood tickles my chin.

I pinched my thumb on my sled. Ouch! It hurt!

All of these things I could feel: **cold, warmth, tickles, pain.** I could feel them because of my skin.

Vocabulary: clothes   warmth

My Skin Warms Me and Cools Me

God gave my skin many wonderful jobs to do to keep me well and strong.

My skin has hundreds of thousands of tiny holes in it. These holes are called **pores.**

When I'm hot, my pores open. I will sweat. This lets the heat get out of my body and cools me off.

When I'm cold, my pores close. No heat will get out. Sometimes I get so cold that my skin gets tight and I shiver. Then I get **"goose-bumps"!**

Taking Care of My Skin

My skin is always making new skin.

When I take a bath, some old skin always rubs off. But some new skin is always there to take its place.

Sometimes my skin gets dirty. Dirt has many germs in it. But these germs will not get into my body, because my skin keeps them out—unless my skin gets cut.

If my skin gets cut, it works even harder. If I wash my cut and keep it clean, my skin will mend itself. In a few weeks, I will not even see the cut.

Something to do!

God gave me five senses. I can **see, hear, smell, taste,** and **feel.**

Write the words where they go.

feeling, sight, smell, taste, hearing

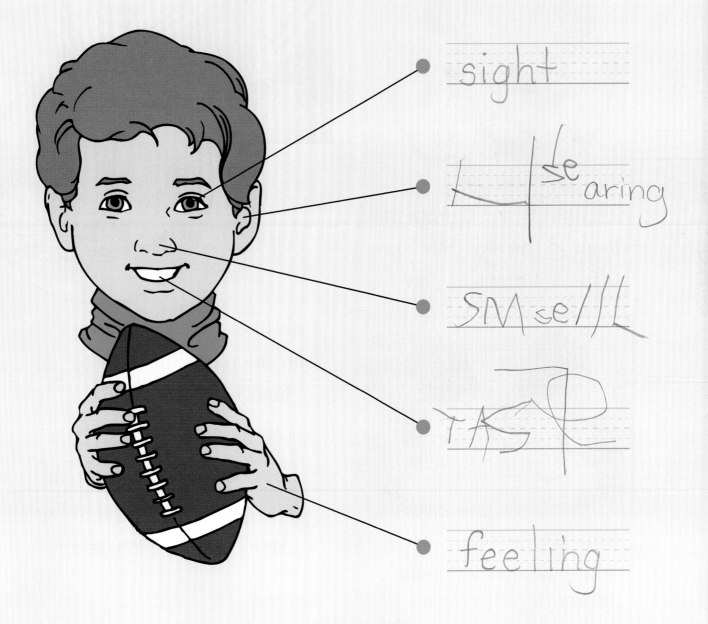

sight

hearing

SMsell

TASTE

feeling

I Am Me!

Kim and Sue are twins. They look alike, but . . .

Kim likes to see flowers and clouds in the sky. Sue likes to see kittens at play.

Kim likes pudding best of all. Sue likes ice cream.

Kim likes to hear raindrops on the roof. Sue likes to hear her mother sing.

God made me different from everyone else. I'm glad I'm me. Aren't you glad you're you?

Vocabulary: pudding

Discovering
My Toys

I like to run and jump and play. God wants me to have the right kind of fun. It will help me grow strong. It will help me have the right kind of thoughts. I must think of the girls and boys I play with.

I have many kinds of toys. I can put them in groups.

Water

Here are some **water toys.**

This is a boat. The water keeps the boat moving.

This is a bathtub toy. It floats.

Vocabulary: thoughts   groups   moving

Air

Air is what makes these toys fun.

Can you tell why air is important to each of these toys? Would they work without air?

Wind

The **wind** helps me to have fun with these toys. Wind is air that moves.

This is a kite. The wind lifts the kite into the air and keeps it there. If the wind stops blowing, the kite will come down.

This is a pinwheel. The wind blows the wheel. The wheel turns. It will go fast if the wind blows hard.

This is a sailboat. The wind blows against the sails and makes the boat move.

Vocabulary: moves   pinwheel

Working Together

Sometimes different things work together to help me have more fun with my toys.

Air fills this toy. Water makes it float.

Air fills these bubbles. The wind carries them away.

Air can be still. When air moves, we have wind. Wind will move the sailboat on top of the water.

Vocabulary: together

Yes, air, wind, and water all work together to help me have fun with my toys.

Do you know what would happen if they did not work together? My toys would not be very much fun, would they?

I am glad that God created all things to work together.

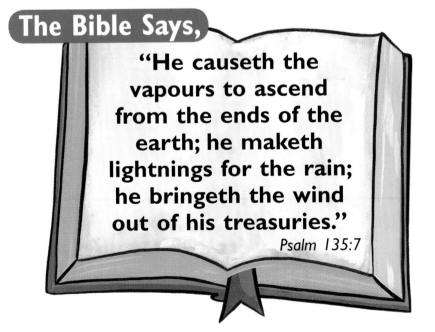

The Bible Says,

"He causeth the vapours to ascend from the ends of the earth; he maketh lightnings for the rain; he bringeth the wind out of his treasuries."
Psalm 135:7

Vocabulary: create—created

 **Something to try!**

Make a balloon jet.

When air moves, it makes other things move, too.
Try this and see!

What you need:

- a balloon

What to do:

1. Blow up the balloon.

With what did you fill it?

2. Pinch the balloon closed and hold it above your head.

3. Let go!

What happened?

The balloon was filled with air. When you let go, the air rushed out. It pushed the balloon the opposite way. A jet plane works this way, too, but it uses very hot gasses.

Vocabulary: opposite

Something to do!

Different things make different toys fun. **Wind** moves some. *Color those toys blue.* **Air** fills some. *Color those toys red.* **Water** floats some. *Color those toys yellow.* Some toys will be two colors.

Wheels

Wheels make other toys fun.

Something to try!

See how wheels help.

Do wheels make it easier to move things? Try this and see!

What you need:

- a toy truck or car with wheels that can come off

What to do:

1. Push the toy across a smooth floor.
2. Take the wheels off and try again.

Which way was easier?

A wheel is a tool that makes work easier. Other tools are ramps and levers.

Vocabulary: easy—easier   lever

Ramps

A ramp can make it easier to move things with wheels and without wheels. Find the ramps.

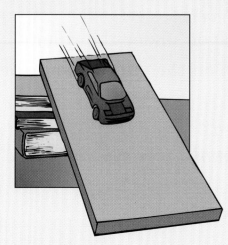

Something to try! ⎯⎯⎯⎯⎯⎯

Have a ramp race.

Can a ramp help things move down faster? Try this and see!

What you need:

- a toy truck or car
- a board
- some books

What to do:

1. Pile some books on the floor.
2. Put one end of the board on the books and the other on the floor. You made a ramp!
3. Put the toy at the top of the ramp.
4. Let go!

What happened?

Will the toy go down faster if you add more books? Try it and see!

Levers

A lever makes it easier to move things, too. With a lever I can make my father go up in the air! With a lever I can open cans.

 **Something to try!**

Make a lever lifter.

Does a lever make it easier to lift something? Try this and see!

What you need:

- a ruler
- a crayon
- a ball of clay

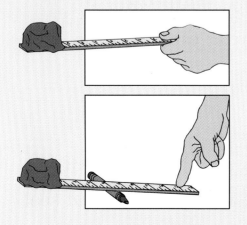

What to do:

1. Press the clay firmly on one end of the ruler.
2. Hold the other end of the ruler.
3. Make the clay go up.

Now make a lever:
1. Put the crayon under the ruler.
2. Push down on the end without the clay.

What happened?
Did the lever make it easier to lift the clay?

Magnets

Do you like to play with a magnet? It is fun to see what a magnet will pick up. Magnets can move things, and they can hold things together.

Magnets make the cars of the train stick together.

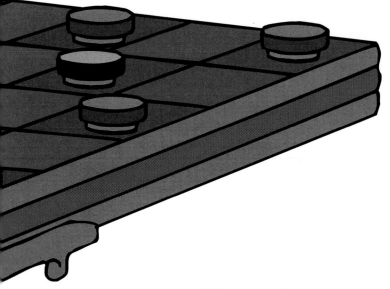

Magnets hold the parts of my travel game on. That helps when the car is moving!

Vocabulary: magnet   iron   travel

 **Something to try!**

Discover what a magnet will pick up.

Magnets pick up some things but not others.
What kinds of things will a magnet pick up?
Try this and see!

What you need:

- magnet
- needle
- paper clip
- pencil
- safety pin
- leaf
- rubber band
- plastic button
- small scissors

What to do:

1. Put everything but the magnet into 2 piles: things you think the magnet will pick up and things you think it will not pick up.

2. Try to pick up each thing with the magnet.

What things did the magnet pick up?

Circle the picture of each thing the magnet picked up.

Something to do!

Tim made a toy boat. He put it in a pan of water. He wants to have fun with it.

How can he make the boat go?
Circle the ways you think will work.

1. He could push it with his finger.

2. He could pull it with a magnet.

3. He could wish for it to go.

4. He could blow on the water.

5. He could blow on the sail.

6. He could blow up a balloon and then let out the air to move the sail.

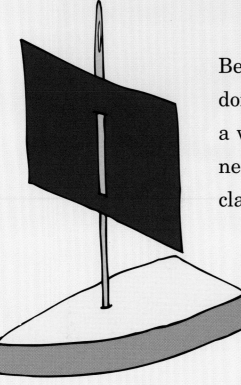

Could you make a boat like Tim's? Be careful with the needle! If you don't have plastic foam, try using half a walnut shell. You can attach the needle to the shell with a little bit of clay or chewing gum.

Discovering **Animals**

Animals are fun. There are so many of them.

Some are

HUGE.

Some are **BIG.**

Some are little.

Some are tiny.

Can you think of others?

Vocabulary: animals

How Do Animals Learn?

Do animals go to school? Who teaches them the things they need to know?

God does. He gave each animal **instincts.** Instincts tell an animal what to do.

Vocabulary: instincts

The Bible Says,

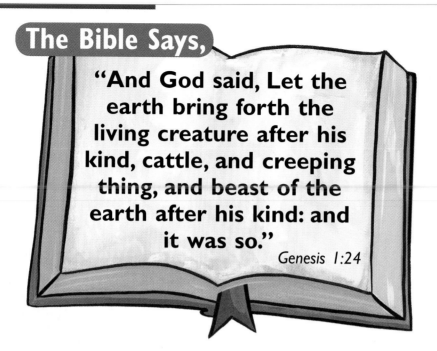

"And God said, Let the earth bring forth the living creature after his kind, cattle, and creeping thing, and beast of the earth after his kind: and it was so."

Genesis 1:24

Each kind of animal is different from every other kind of animal. This is God's plan.

God placed a special seed in each kind of animal so that animals would never change into another kind of animal.

Kittens will always grow up to be cats.

Puppies will always grow up to be dogs.

Vocabulary: creature

Discovering Baby Animals

Some baby animals are **born.** Almost all animals that are born drink milk from their mothers. Their mothers will take care of them until they get big enough to catch food.

When baby kittens are born, they cannot see or walk. Mother Cat takes very good care of them. When they get bigger, they like to play, but they must still stay close to their mother.

Baby bears are born in winter while Mother Bear is in her cave. When they are born, the bear cubs are no bigger than kittens. They are blind and helpless. They eat and sleep and grow for many weeks beside their mother.

Vocabulary: enough   blind
helpless

A mother mouse can have as many as nine babies at one time. A mouse is no bigger than a jellybean when he is born.

A baby bat holds on to his mother's fur as she flies. When the baby grows bigger, the mother bat hangs her babies upside down in their cave-home while she gets food. Then she comes back to the cave to feed the babies.

A whale is not a fish. A baby whale is as big as an elephant. When he is grown up, he will be as big as 30 to 50 elephants put together.

Vocabulary: babies   elephant

Babies Who Live in Pockets

The kangaroo and opossum have a pocket or **pouch** for their babies. These babies are very tiny and very helpless. If they did not have a nice, warm pouch to grow in, they would die.

Baby opossums

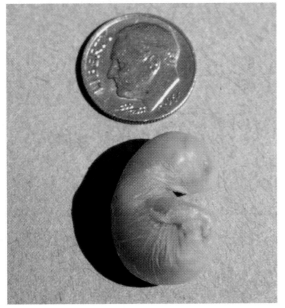

These are baby opossums. As many as 18 or 20 are born at one time. They are so tiny that several could fit in a teaspoon. Do you see why they need their mother's pouch? They cannot see. They have no hair.

Vocabulary: kangaroo   opossum

The pouch keeps them from getting lost. It keeps them warm. They drink milk from their mother while they are in the pouch. After eight weeks, they come out of the pouch and ride around on their mother's back.

Do you know what a baby opossum will look like when he grows up?

Baby kangaroos

A baby kangaroo is called a joey. He is only one inch long when he is born. He is not very strong at all. His mother keeps him in her pouch. The pouch keeps the baby safe for about three months. While the baby is in the pouch, he rests, drinks milk, and grows strong.

Then one day—Pop! Out comes the baby kangaroo's head to look around. Sometimes he reaches down and takes a bite of grass. When he is a little older, he will hop in and out of his mother's pouch.

Vocabulary: joey   months

What do YOU think?

Do you think baby kangaroos and opossums could live if God had not given their mothers a pouch? Why not?

Something to do!

Write a word to answer the question.

1. Will a baby bat grow up to be a mouse?

2. Does a baby opossum live in a pouch?

3. Who teaches animals?

Circle the right word.

1. Animals that are born drink (**water, milk**) from their mothers.

2. Their (**mothers, friends**) will look after them.

Babies That Hatch

Some animals **hatch** from eggs. Each animal has a different sized egg. Some eggs are different colors. Most baby animals that hatch from eggs do not drink milk. They eat other things.

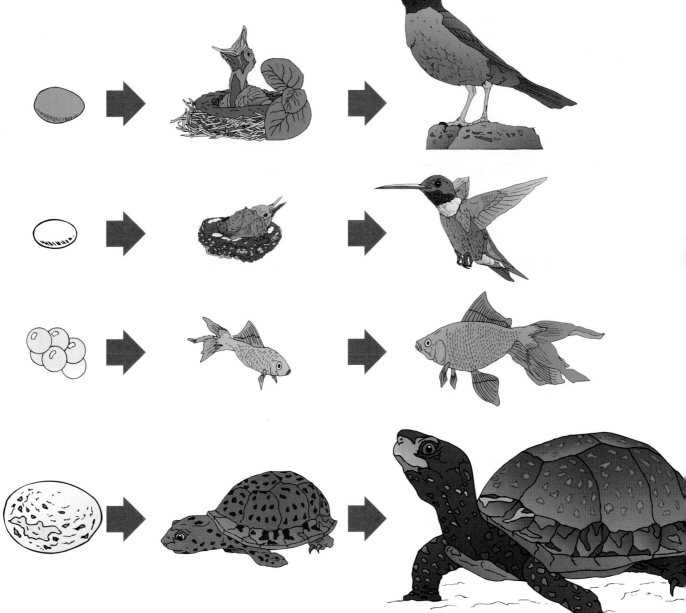

Do you know what each of these animals will look like when he grows up?

duckling

chick

alligator

tadpole

Frogs

Some babies change very much as they grow up. At first, they do not look like their parents at all.

Here is how a frog changes from egg to tadpole to frog.

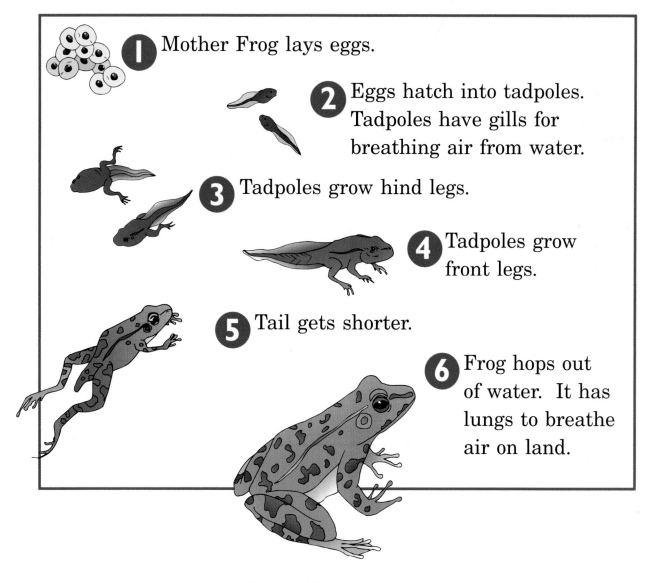

1 Mother Frog lays eggs.

2 Eggs hatch into tadpoles. Tadpoles have gills for breathing air from water.

3 Tadpoles grow hind legs.

4 Tadpoles grow front legs.

5 Tail gets shorter.

6 Frog hops out of water. It has lungs to breathe air on land.

Vocabulary: parents

 **Something to try!**

Grow a frog.

Can you raise a tadpole and watch it change into a frog?
Try this and see!

What you need:

- tadpoles or frog eggs (from pond or nature store)
- pond water (or tap water that you let sit for 2 days)
- water plants (from pond or pet store)
- gravel
- big glass or plastic jar or bowl with top
- freshwater fish food (from pet store)
- rocks

What to do:

1. Put jar where it will get some sunlight.
2. Put gravel into jar and carefully add water.
3. Add plants and tadpoles or eggs. Put lid on.
4. About 4 days after tadpoles hatch, begin feeding a pinch of fish food each day.
5. Wait and watch. It may take tadpoles a few months to change into frogs.
6. When tadpoles start to become frogs, add rocks so they can climb out of water.
7. Watch the frogs for a little while and then let them go near a pond.

What things did you see happen?

Number the pictures 1, 2, 3, 4, 5 to tell what happens first, second, third, fourth, and last. Start with the egg.

Something to do!

All babies need to grow. They will change
as they grow, but they will always look just like
their parents after they are grown.

Draw a line from the mother to her baby.

Something to do!

Some animals change very much. They do not
look like their mother at all when they are young.

Draw a line from the baby to its mother.

God's Wonderful Plan

God made everything for a reason. Each kind of animal is different. God made each kind of animal for a special reason. Because of this, God gave each animal special feet, eyes, teeth, mouths, necks, and even noses. If it were not for these special things, each kind of animal would die.

This is all a part of God's wonderful plan for our world.

God Made the Elephant

The elephant has very little eyes. He cannot see very far.

So God gave the elephant very big ears. He can hear much better than I can. He can even hear a leaf fall from the tree.

 **Something to try!** _____

Discover how big ears help an elephant hear.

Do the elephant's big ears really help it hear better?
Try this and see!

What you need:

- a piece of tablet paper
- a clock or watch that ticks
- a friend

What to do:

1. Ask your friend to stand far away with the clock and to walk closer to you.

2. When you hear the clock tick, raise your hand so your friend will stop.

3. Roll the paper to make a cone with a little hole at one end.

4. Put the small end near your ear.

5. Ask your friend to move away again with the clock and then walk closer.

Where was your friend this time when you heard the clock?

Your "big ear" helped you collect more of the shaking air from the clock's ticks.

The elephant's trunk

God also gave the elephant a very long nose. It is called a **trunk.** He uses his trunk for many things. The elephant can smell much better than I can. He can smell danger.

He also uses his trunk as a hand to take food to his mouth. The trunk is not his mouth. His trunk is so long, he can reach up into a tree or all the way down to the ground to get his dinner.

Vocabulary: danger

The elephant uses his trunk to bring water to his mouth for a drink.

If he gets too hot, the elephant draws water up his trunk and gives himself a shower. He might give **YOU** a shower if you get too close!

If a baby elephant is bad, Mother Elephant spanks him with her trunk! Ouch!

You might think the elephant's trunk must be tired at the end of the day. But God planned for the elephant's trunk to do all that work. He gave the elephant's trunk thousands and thousands of muscles.

The elephant can pick up a very big tree with his trunk. He can also pick up a little peanut.

Isn't the trunk a wonderful part of God's plan for the elephant?

Vocabulary: muscles

The elephant's tusks

Do you wonder why God gave the elephant **tusks?** They are important too.

The elephant uses these tusks to dig up the roots of trees. Then he can pick up the tree with his trunk.

His tusks help him to fight if any wild animal or danger comes. So his tusks are God's way of protecting him.

Vocabulary: protecting

The elephant's feet are flat to keep him from sinking into the ground. Why do you think God planned for the elephant to have heavy, round legs? *to support his heavy body*

What is Wrong?

1. Could the elephant live like this? Why not?

2. What special things did God give to the elephant to help him live?

God Made Ducks

Ducks love the water. They can swim well.
Do you know why ducks are such good swimmers?

All ducks have a **sac** of oil above their tails.
This sac oils their feathers. This makes the duck
waterproof and helps him swim.

Vocabulary: feathers

 **Something to try!** _____

Find out how oil helps a duck.

*How does oil from the duck's oil sac make the
duck waterproof? Try this and see!*

What you need:

- piece of paper
- small cup of water
- drop of cooking oil

What to do:

1. Put the drop of oil on one part of the paper.
2. Sprinkle a little water on the paper—some on the oil part and some on the other part.

Do you see the difference?

Oil and water do not mix. Oil makes water
slide right off the duck's back.

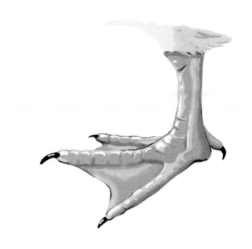

God also gave the ducks two paddles to make them move quickly through the water. Can you guess what they are? They are **webbed feet.**

If their feet were not webbed, they could not swim fast. Then they could not get away from other animals that would like to eat them.

Vocabulary: guess

The duck has a flat **bill.** The bill has edges that look like tiny teeth.

Why is the duck's bill flat? Why does he have "teeth"?

God knew the duck would eat tadpoles and worms and things in the mud. The bill is a tool for catching food. The little "teeth" keep the food from slipping out. The "teeth" help him to pull up grass. The duck would starve without his bill and his "teeth."

Vocabulary: edges

Something to do!

Finish the puzzle.

1➡ A duck loves to _____.

2⬇ An oil _____ keeps
   the duck dry.

3⬇ A duck eats with his _____.

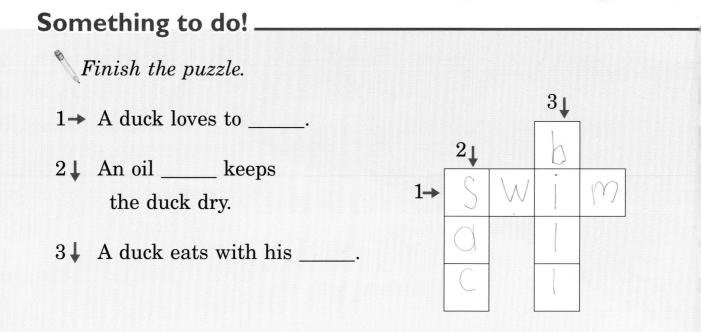

God Made Turtles

A turtle moves very slowly. He is so slow that just about anything could catch him. So God gave him a shell to protect him. When danger comes, he pulls himself inside the shell.

A turtle has no teeth. So God gave him jaws that have sharp edges.

How does a turtle know when to go into his shell? He can feel the ground pounding. God thought about all of the turtle's needs when He made him.

After the mother turtle lays her eggs, she leaves them and never comes back. The sun shines on the sand and keeps the eggs warm until they hatch. When the baby turtles hatch, they seem to know just what to do. Can you tell who taught them?

Land turtles have short feet with blunt claws. They use their claws to tear up food. They also use them to scratch sand over their eggs.

Water turtles have webbed feet or flippers to help them swim. They can swim away fast if danger comes.

Do you remember?

Mark the O under the right answer.

1. A turtle is very ___?___.

   slow   **fast**
   ◉   ○

2. His ___?___ protects him.

   hair   **shell**
   ○   ◉

3. Baby turtles ___?___.

   hatch from eggs   **are born**
   ◉   ○

4. A water turtle has ___?___.

   blunt claws   **webbed feet or flippers**
   ○   ◉

God Made the Owl

There are many kinds of owls.

One of the first things we notice about owls are their eyes. An owl's eyes take up more room in his head than his brain does. God planned for the owl to see things both far away and close.

God gave the owl extra eyelids. He uses them to protect his eyes when he is flying. They are his "safety glasses."

Vocabulary: notice   extra

Most birds have eyes on the side of their head. But owls have eyes in the front. This helps them to quickly spot and catch small animals that move very fast.

I can move my eyes, but an owl cannot. So when Mr. Owl wants to see something coming, he turns his head without turning his body. He can turn his head much farther than I can turn mine.

The owl's feathers are very strong. The edges of the feathers are short and soft. Because of this, when Mr. Owl flies, his wings will not make a sound. He can sneak up on things he likes to eat without making a sound. He likes to eat mice, rats, rabbits, and sometimes bugs.

The owl's feet are special, too. They are called **talons.** They are very sharp. He kills his dinner with them. Then he grabs his dinner with his talons and carries it back to his nest.

What is Wrong?

1. Could the owl live this way? Why not?

2. What special things did God give to the owl to help him live?

Vocabulary: talons   carries

Discovering Insects

Insects are animals, too. They are very important to us.

Insects give us honey.

Insects give us silk.

Insects help trees and plants to make seeds.

Insects are food for many animals.

What Is an Insect?

All insects, when grown, have six legs.

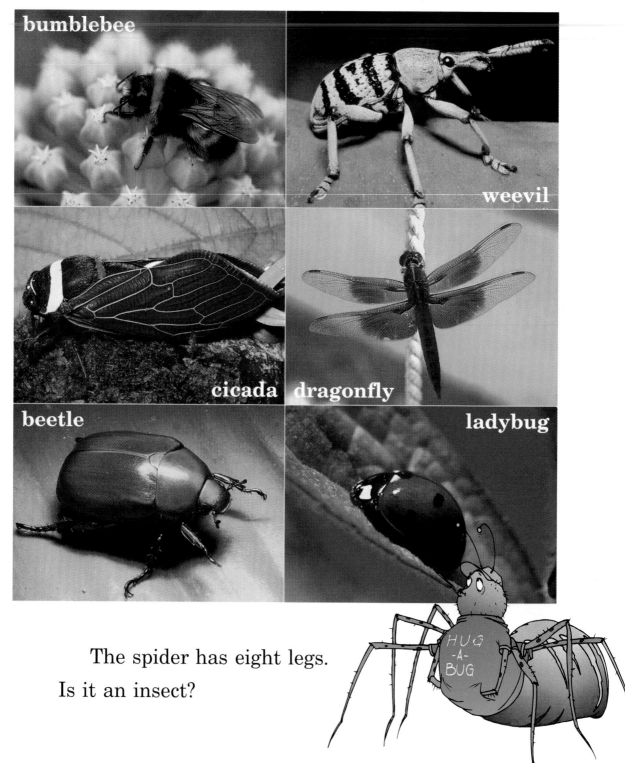

bumblebee

weevil

cicada dragonfly

beetle

ladybug

The spider has eight legs.

Is it an insect?

HUG -A- BUG

How Many Insects Do You Know?

God made the insects in all shapes and sizes. Insects have many different colors. See how many of these insects you know.

A caterpillar has many legs. Why is it an insect? Turn the page to find out!

 **Something to try!** _____

Watch a caterpillar change.

A caterpillar started life as a tiny egg. A caterpillar has many legs, but it is just a baby insect. It will change into a lovely insect with six legs. Try this and see!

What you need:

- a big jar
- a lid with holes punched in it (Ask an adult to punch the holes.)
- a caterpillar
- some leaves from the plant you found the caterpillar on
- twigs for the caterpillar to crawl on
- a field guide to butterflies and moths
- a hand lens

What to do:

1. Put the leaves and twigs into the jar.
2. Add the caterpillar.
3. Screw the lid on.
4. Put a few drops of water on the leaves every day. Add new leaves when needed.
5. Watch the caterpillar eat and EAT!

What happens to the caterpillar?
   It will turn into a pupa and go to sleep. After many days, a butterfly or moth will come out.

How many legs will the butterfly or moth have?
6. Let the butterfly or moth go where you found the caterpillar.

Something to do!

Number the pictures 1, 2, 3, 4 to show what happens first, next, third, and last. Start with the egg.

3

4

1

2

Something to try!

Make an insect zoo.

Can you have a zoo small enough to keep in your room? Try this and see!

What you need:

- jars with lids
- a field guide to insects
- hand lens

What to do:

1. Ask an adult to punch holes in the jar lids for you.

2. Look for insects outside.

3. Put one in each jar, along with leaves from the plant it was on.

4. Put the lid on quickly.

5. Try to find your zoo animals in the field guide.

6. Watch your insects for a day or two, and then let them go where you found them.

Something to do!

Draw a line from the insect to its name.

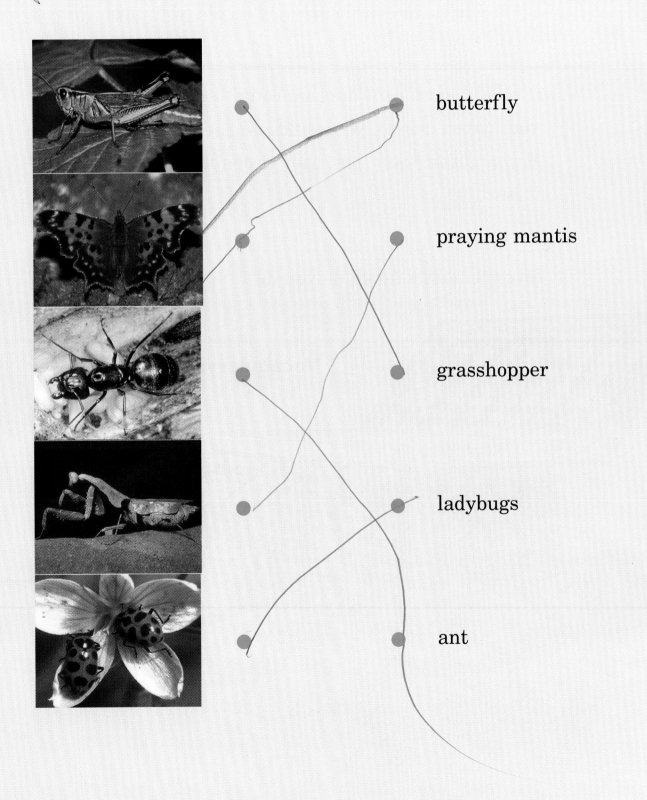

butterfly

praying mantis

grasshopper

ladybugs

ant

God Made Ants

If you have ever been on a picnic, you most likely have had some guests you did not invite.

They were tiny, but you could see them. If you looked closely, you could see they had six legs. If you got in their way, they probably bit you, and it hurt.

Who were your guests? They were ants. Ants love picnics as much as you do.

Vocabulary: guests   probably   crumbs

If you left some crumbs, an ant may have carried them away. She can carry things up to six times as big as she is.

Can you carry things six times bigger than you? No, you do not need to. But the ant does.

The ants you saw on your picnic are called **workers.** Workers do all of the work for the ant family, or **colony.** The ant colony can have thousands of ants, so the workers are very busy.

Vocabulary: colony   busy

What Do Ants Eat?

The workers must find food for everyone back at the ant nest. Grown-up ants' throats are too small to eat food. Only the babies eat food. So your picnic crumbs are going to feed the ant babies.

The grown-up ants drink juices which they squeeze from fruit and other things. When an ant finds some juice to take back to the nest, she puts it in an extra stomach God gave her. This stomach is just for carrying juice back to the nest.

Vocabulary: stomach

The worker has many other jobs, too. She must take care of the queen ant, all of the babies, and all of the queen's eggs.

The workers lick the eggs and keep them clean. If the room the eggs are in gets too damp, the workers will move the eggs to a dry room. If it is a very hot day, the workers will move the eggs to a cool room.

As the queen ant lays more eggs, the workers build more rooms in the nest.

Some rooms are for the eggs. Some rooms are for the babies after they hatch. Some rooms are to store food. Sometimes there is even a room for trash.

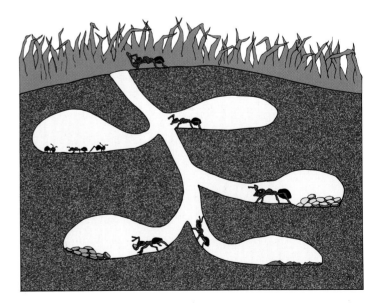

Vocabulary: build

The worker is also a good housekeeper. She keeps the nest very clean. Some colonies have workers that will even mow the grass. Their lawnmower is their jaws.

If danger comes, the workers are the ones to fight the enemy.

The workers are very busy little ants, aren't they? God wants us to be busy, too.

Vocabulary: housekeeper   lawnmower   enemy

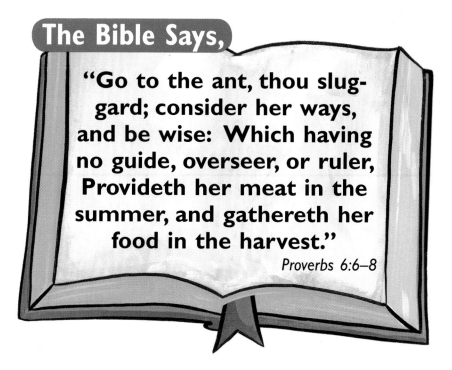

The Bible Says,

"Go to the ant, thou sluggard; consider her ways, and be wise: Which having no guide, overseer, or ruler, Provideth her meat in the summer, and gathereth her food in the harvest."

Proverbs 6:6–8

The Queen Ant

There is only one **queen ant** in each ant colony. If any other queen ant hatches, she must soon leave the nest and start a family of her own.

The queen's only job is to lay eggs. Could a queen ant's eggs hatch into bees? Why not?

Does the queen tell the workers what to do? No, they seem to know what to do.

Who told all the ants what to do? God, their Creator.

Vocabulary: Creator

 **Something to try!**

Make an ant farm.

Can you catch some ants and watch them work? Try this and see!

What you need:

- a large jar with small holes punched in lid
- black paper cut to put around jar
- tape
- dirt
- bits of fruit, vegetables, and meat for food
- hand lens

What to do:

1. Fill the jar with dirt, leaving about 2" at top empty.
2. Find some ants and put them into the jar. Look for one very big ant. She is the queen. Put her in, too. Try to find eggs to put in, too.
3. Add some food.
4. Put the lid on.
5. Tape the black paper around the jar.
6. Take the paper off when you want to watch the ants.

What things can you see the ants do?

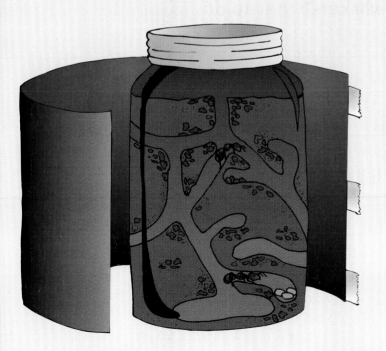

Do you remember?

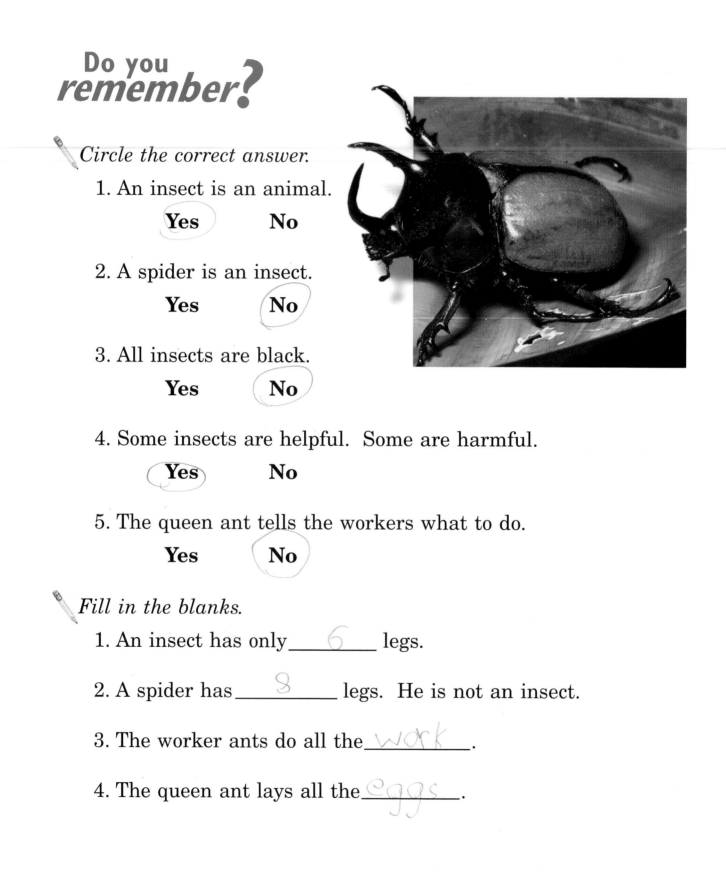

Circle the correct answer.

1. An insect is an animal.

   (Yes)   No

2. A spider is an insect.

   Yes   (No)

3. All insects are black.

   Yes   (No)

4. Some insects are helpful. Some are harmful.

   (Yes)   No

5. The queen ant tells the workers what to do.

   Yes   (No)

Fill in the blanks.

1. An insect has only ___6___ legs.

2. A spider has ___8___ legs. He is not an insect.

3. The worker ants do all the ___work___.

4. The queen ant lays all the ___eggs___.

Discovering **Plants**

Plants are a very important part of God's plan for our world. We need plants to live. Without plants, there could be no life at all.

We Need Plants to Live

There are many things we enjoy and need. But we could not have them without plants.

We need milk to grow strong. The cow eats grass. She needs this grass to make milk.

Meg has a new cotton dress. Cotton comes from a plant.

Peter has a coat made from wool. Wool comes from sheep. The sheep must eat plants to make the wool.

Vocabulary: cotton

We like ham. Ham comes from pigs. Pigs need to eat plants.

Most food that God gives us comes from plants. Without them, we would not be very strong.

When we get sick, we need medicine to help us get well. Some medicines are made from plants.

Vocabulary: medicine

Animals use plants to make homes.

We use plants to make our homes, too.

We need plants more than they need us.

How many kinds of plants are there? There are hundreds of thousands of kinds of plants.

Some are huge.

Some are so tiny you cannot see them.

Things to Look For

Some plants look almost alike. Some do not. But most of the common plants have **roots, stems, leaves,** and **flowers** or **cones.**

Roots, stems, and leaves move water from one part of the plant to another.

The flower is the part of the plant that makes the **seeds.** Seeds grow into new plants.

Some plants, like pine trees, have cones instead of flowers.

Each part is important.

cone

Vocabulary: common   instead

 **Something to try!** _____

Find a baby plant and watch it grow.

Did you know that a bean is a seed? It has a baby plant inside and food to help the baby plant grow. Can you find the baby plant and watch it grow? Try this and see!

What you need:

- 5 dried lima beans
- a glass of water
- paper towels, folded
- a clear cup or small jar

What to do:

1. Soak the beans in the water overnight.
2. Take one bean out. With your fingers, take the bean's coat off.
3. Open the bean to see the two parts.

Do you see the baby bean plant?

4. Find the parts that will be leaves and roots. The rest is food for the baby plant.

5. Put paper towels around the inside of the cup or jar.
6. Put 4 beans between the towels and cup.
7. Put the cup in a warm place and keep a little water in the bottom.
8. In a few days your beans will sprout. Watch for a few more days.

Which way do the stems grow? Which way do the roots grow?

Note: Let your seeds grow in the cup for a while. On page 120 you will learn how to plant them.

Flowers, Seeds, and Fruits

It is the **flower's** job to make seeds for new plants.

We eat many things that come from flowers. They are called **fruits.**

We also eat some **seeds** that flowers make.

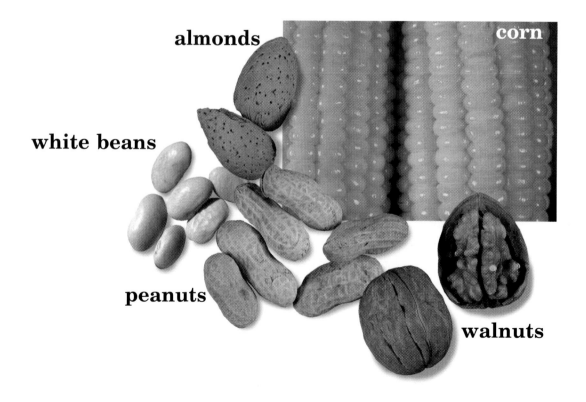

almonds

corn

white beans

peanuts

walnuts

Plants make seeds so that new plants can grow. There are many kinds of apples, but an apple seed always grows into an apple tree. It could never become a cherry tree. This is God's plan.

God placed a special kind of seed into each kind of plant. God likes things the way He made them, and He planned for them to stay that way.

HANDS ON activity **Something to try!**

Make some funny planters.

What you need:

- eggshell halves
- colored marking pens
- empty egg carton
- potting soil
- rye grass seeds
- water

What to do:

1. Draw funny faces on the eggshells.
2. Put the shells into the egg carton.
3. Add potting soil.
4. Add some rye grass seeds.
5. Sprinkle a little water on top each day.

What happens?

Note: If you don't have eggshells, try planting seeds on a sponge. Be sure to keep it damp! Other seeds to try are cress, mustard, and clover.

Roots

Roots are not very pretty, but they have a very big job. They grow underground and drink in water and **minerals** from the soil. They hold the plant in the ground.

We eat the roots of many vegetables.

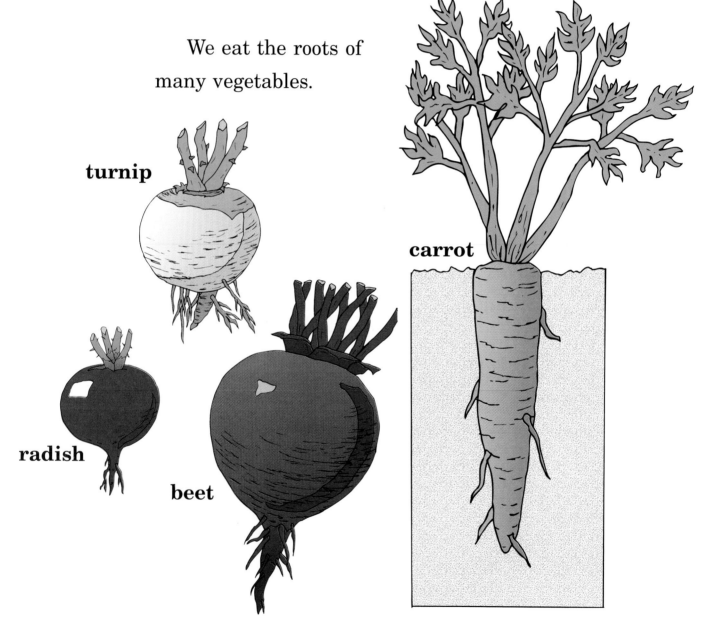

Vocabulary: minerals   vegetables

 **Something to try!**

Grow a plant from a root.

Plants are so important to our life that God made many ways for them to grow. You know that a plant will grow from a seed. Did you know that you can grow a new plant from part of a root? Try this and see!

What you need:

- top of carrot root (Ask an adult to cut it for you.)
- dish
- water

What to do:

1. Put the carrot into the dish with the cut side down.
2. Cover most of it with water.
3. Change the water every day.
4. Wait and watch for about a week.

What grows from the top of the carrot?
What grows from the bottom?

Stems

Stems move the water from the roots to the leaves.

We eat some stems of plants.

asparagus   **celery**

 **Something to try!**

Watch water rise up a stem.

A stem has long tubes in it. Water goes up the tubes from the roots to the stems. Try this and see!

What you need:

- stalk of celery with leaves (Ask an adult to cut the stalk about 1 inch from its base.)
- tall glass or jar
- water
- 1 tsp. red food coloring

What to do:

1. Pour 1 inch water into glass or jar.
2. Add food coloring.
3. Put celery in, cut side down.
4. Watch to see what happens.

How long does it take the colored water to reach the leaves?

5. Ask an adult to cut across the stalk again so you can see the tubes.

Leaves

It is the **leaves'** job to make food for the plant.

We eat some leaves of plants.

spinach

cabbage

lettuce

Something to do!

Look for leaves on trees and other plants. Collect one leaf from each plant. How many different shapes did you find? You can preserve the leaves by putting them between paper towels. Put some newspapers over the towels. Put heavy books on top of the newspapers. Leave them for 3 weeks.

We are not plants. But as we go on discovering God's world, let us keep our hearts like gardens.

Kind hearts are the gardens,
Kind words are the roots,
Kind thoughts are the flowers,
Kind deeds are the fruits.

Take care of your garden
And keep out the weeds;
Fill it with sunshine,
Kind words and good deeds.

Henry W. Longfellow

The Bible Says,

"He causeth the grass to grow for the cattle, and herb for the service of man: that he may bring forth food out of the earth."

Psalm 104:14

Something to do!

We cannot eat all plants. God made some of them just for us to enjoy. Use the key to finish coloring these flowers.

Key

1 = **purple**
2 = **red**
3 = yellow
4 = **pink**
5 = **green**

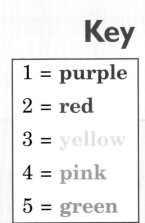

Do you *remember*?

Circle the correct answer.

1. The ___?___ drinks water from the soil and keeps the plant from falling over.

   root   **stem**   **leaves**   **flower**

2. The ___?___ moves water from the roots to the leaves.

   root   **stem**   **leaf**   **flower**

3. The ___?___ make the plant's food.

   root   **stem**   **leaves**   **flower**

4. The ___?___ makes the seeds.

   root   **stem**   **leaves**   **flower**

5. A peach seed becomes a ___?___.

   apple tree   **peach tree**   **rose**

Something to do!

These pretty flowers are pansies.

✏️ *Write the names of the parts on the lines.*

Discovering **Seasons**

God gives us four seasons to enjoy each year.
They are . . .

Winter

December
January
February

Spring

March
April
May

Summer

June

July

August

Fall

September

October

November

Do you know what season comes after fall?

Year after year, God is faithful to send us the seasons.

Winter, spring, summer, fall— God our Father brings them all!

Winter—
A Time for Rest

Winter is the coldest season of the year.
Many places have ice and snow. Days are short,
and nights are long. What is winter like where
you live?

Some trees keep their green leaves all winter.
These are **evergreen** trees. A Christmas tree is
an evergreen tree. Other
trees are brown and bare
all winter long. If you look
closely, though, you will see
buds on their twigs.

God planned the world so
we would always have plants.
Many small plants die in the
winter, but they leave their
seeds behind. The seeds rest
in the ground until spring.

Vocabulary: Christmas

 **Something to try!**

Bring some twigs to life.

Trees and shrubs have buds on their branches all winter long. The buds have hard covers. New leaves and flowers lie safely inside the buds, waiting for the sunshine and rains of spring.

What will happen if you bring some brown twigs inside and give them water? What is inside their buds? Try this and see!

What you need:

- some twigs from trees or shrubs (They should have buds, but no leaves or flowers. Examples: apple, cherry, willow, beech, ash, maple, and oak.)
- a glass or vase
- warm water
- a razor blade (Have an adult use it.)
- a hand lens

What to do:

1. Ask an adult to help cut the twigs from the plant and peel or mash the thick ends where the cut was made.
2. Ask an adult to cut a few buds open with a razor blade so you can see what is inside. Look closely with the hand lens.

What do you see?

3. Put the twigs in a glass of warm water in a warm, light spot indoors.
4. Change the water every 2 days.
5. Wait and watch a few weeks.

What happens?

Some animals **hibernate** all winter. They sleep deeply in burrows or dens or nests under the leaves and snow. Snakes, turtles, and frogs hibernate. So do woodchucks, chipmunks, bats, and bumblebee queens. God gave these animals the instinct to hibernate. Other animals take long naps, but they wake up to eat or to go outside. Mother bears nap, eat, and have their cubs in winter. Fish live quietly in the water under the ice.

Vocabulary: hibernate   burrows

 **Something to try!**

Find air in water and soil.

All animals need air to breathe. How do fish get air under water? How do animals get air when they hibernate? Try this and see!

What you need:

- two clear glasses
- water
- soil

What to do:

1. Put water in one glass and look at it every ten minutes.

Do you see air bubbles in the water? If not, put the glass in a pan of warm water.

2. Fill the other glass halfway with soil.

3. Put water in the glass.

Do you see bubbles come up?

The bubbles that you see are air bubbles. There is air in soil. There is air in water, even under the ice. God gave the animals what they need to live, even in the winter!

 **Something to try!** _____

Make a bird feeder.

Some birds fly to warmer places for the winter. We say they migrate. Other birds stay in the cold. Can you give the birds some food to eat? Try this and see!

What you need:

- a plastic cup
- bird seed
- peanut butter
- string

What to do:

1. Mix the bird seed into the peanut butter.

2. Put it into the cup.

3. Ask an adult to punch holes in the cup for the string and for the birds to eat from, and to help you hang your feeder outside where you can watch.

Do birds come to eat?
Can you learn their names?

Vocabulary: migrate

Spring— A Time for New Life

In spring, we have more sunlight each day. It rains often. Seeds that were resting in the cold winter ground have warmth and water, and they start to grow. Buds open on the trees and shrubs, and spring flowers bloom. When do flowers start to bloom where you live?

Animals that were hibernating wake up. Many baby animals are born. Migrating birds begin to return and build nests. We like to hear them sing. It's time to plant our gardens. God has given the world new life!

Vocabulary: hibernating   migrating

 **Something to try!** _____

Plant a bean garden.

Do you still have your bean seeds growing in a glass or jar? They have used up most of the food that was stored in the seed. Now they need food from the soil, water, and sunlight. Can you bring springtime to your seedlings? Try this and see!

What you need:

- your baby bean plants (seed-lings)
- 3 pots
- potting soil
- water
- a sunny spot or a plant light

What to do:

1. Put potting soil into the 3 pots.
2. Plant one seedling in each pot. Leave one in the glass with paper towels so you can see the difference.
3. Put the pots in the sun or under the plant light.
4. Sprinkle just a little water on the soil each day.
5. Watch for a few days.

Are your seedlings growing? What is happening to the seedling with no soil?

Try putting one pot in a refrigerator. What season will this be like? Put another in a warm closet. Water both plants every day. Which plant grows better? Does the plant in the light grow best of all? Do you see why God gives us spring?

Summer— A Time to Grow

In summertime the days are long and the nights are short. It is hot in many places. How hot is summer where you live? Have you visited any place where summer is hotter? Have you visited any place where it is cooler? Are summers rainy or dry where you live?

In summer, fruits begin to grow on the trees. Vegetables grow on farms and in gardens. The baby animals grow, too, and learn new things. We can find many insects on hot summer days.

Vocabulary: vegetables

Fall—
A Time to Get Ready

In fall the days get cooler and shorter. On many trees the leaves turn yellow, red, orange, or brown. Then the leaves drop to the ground. They will make a blanket on the ground for the cold winter. When winter comes, snow may fall to make an extra blanket. The fallen leaves will decay in the soil and become food for spring plants. This is all part of God's plan.

Fall is a busy time of year! As flowers fade, fruits and seeds get ripe. Birds and other animals gather the fruits and seeds. They are getting ready for winter.

Vocabulary: decay

Some birds migrate south to warmer places in the fall. God gives them the instinct to migrate at just the right time.

Jays, woodpeckers, squirrels, and field mice hide seeds in the ground and in trees so they will have food for the winter. Seeds that they forget to eat will grow into new plants in the spring. Some animals find a place to hibernate for the winter. The animals know just what to do. God has planned it that way. As days get colder, winter begins, and the year starts all over again.

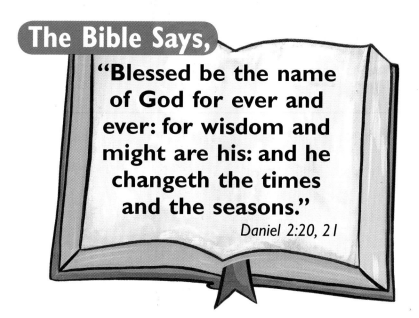

The Bible Says,

"Blessed be the name of God for ever and ever: for wisdom and might are his: and he changeth the times and the seasons."

Daniel 2:20, 21

A Sunflower's Year

1. **Fall.** Birds eat seeds from a dried sunflower head. One seed drops to the ground.

2. **Winter.** The seed rests on the ground.

3. **Spring.** Rain waters the seed, and it sends a root down into the soil.

4. **Spring.** The seed's shoot grows up toward the warm sun.

5. **Spring.** The baby plant grows.

6. **Late spring.** The sunflower plant is now taller than you. It grows a flower bud.

7. **Summer.** The buds open. The sunflower is now full grown. What a pretty sight!

What do you think will happen next? Maybe you could plant some sunflower seeds in your yard and watch them grow.

A Squirrel's Year

1. **Fall.** A gray squirrel is busy gathering nuts and acorns from the trees. She eats all she can and buries the others to save for winter.

2. **Winter.** The squirrel builds a sturdy winter nest in an oak tree. She weaves twigs, grass, leaves, and bark together to keep cold winds and rain out. She stays here at night and on very stormy days. Other days she scampers out and digs up her nuts. In late winter she adds a soft lining of moss or torn bark to the nest. Soon three baby squirrels are born. They are hairless, blind, and helpless. They snuggle up to their mother and drink her warm milk. Soon their fur will grow, and their eyes and ears will open.

3. **Spring.** The baby squirrels grow. When they are a month old, they make short trips outside the nest to explore. The mother squirrel teaches them the best paths to follow. She shows them how to scamper through the treetops and find tender buds and seeds to eat. She shows them how to use their fluffy tails for umbrellas as the spring rains fall.

4. **Summer.** The babies are on their own now. Each makes a nest in its own tree. The mother makes a summer nest, too. It is not snug and warm like the winter nest. It lets the cooling breezes in. She feasts all summer on mushrooms, beetles, caterpillars, flowers, and fruits. Sometimes she raids a cornfield. Soon fall will come again. Then what will she do?

Do you have a squirrel in your yard? If she eats all the food from your bird feeder, why not give her a special treat instead? She just loves corn-on-the-cob! Don't you?

Do you remember?

1. Choose a place to start. Write 1, 2, 3, 4 to show the right order.

Spring 1

Fall 3

Winter 4

Summer 2

*2. Read the clues. Draw a line from the clues to
   the right season.*

Clues   **Seasons**

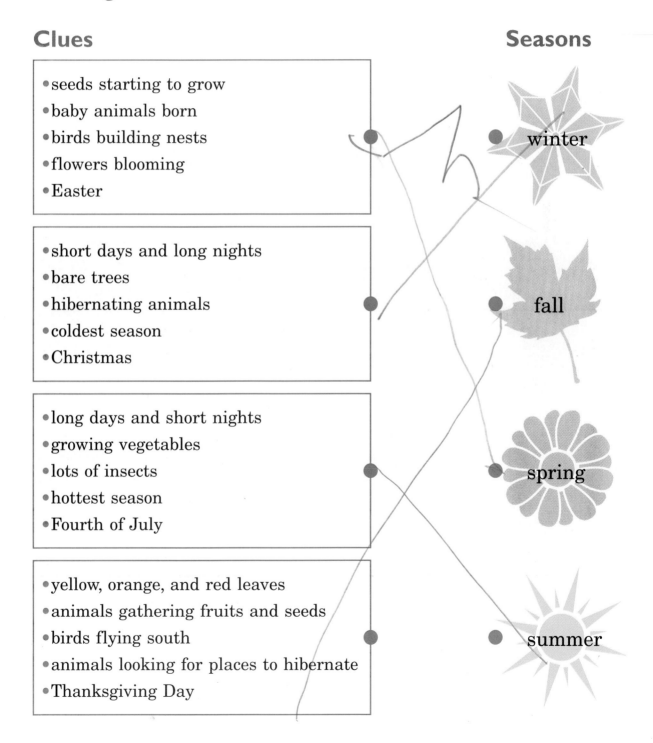

- seeds starting to grow
- baby animals born
- birds building nests
- flowers blooming
- Easter

- short days and long nights
- bare trees
- hibernating animals
- coldest season
- Christmas

- long days and short nights
- growing vegetables
- lots of insects
- hottest season
- Fourth of July

- yellow, orange, and red leaves
- animals gathering fruits and seeds
- birds flying south
- animals looking for places to hibernate
- Thanksgiving Day

winter

fall

spring

summer

"The earth is full of thy riches."

Psalm 104:24